To: My ,
Love, peace, & Blessing !

Riches of Life

Mary F. Lenox

POEMS

MARY F. LENOX

Compilation Copyright © 2019
TBL Publishers
San Diego, CA

First Printing, September 2019

ISBN 978-0-578-54700-8

LCCN: 2019911404

Book Design: Lynn Winston/Powell Graphics & Communication

Cover Photo: Leonid Tit

Table of Contents

Nature   **59**

Acknowledgments

Conversations

Welcome

I knocked on the door of life
Waiting for it to let me in
Not realizing that it was already open
Waiting for me to enter
To bloom into the one I've become
Seeing the sun looking at me
I began to see with my inner vision
The light of love welcoming me into life
I discovered my gifts as I
Walked the shores of lakes, bays, and seas
Each dawn
I rise and answer the call of fresh blessings
Here
There
Everywhere
Ever grateful to say yes
To the Spirit of life

Space

As I look back over my life
I realize that I wanted to grow up in the slow lane
Looking at flowers and trees growing
Reading books in the corner of a room
Wanting solitude and silence each day
Giving space for my thoughts to bloom
Then leisurely sharing them with my mother
At the kitchen table
Listening to my mother and aunt
Whispering secrets unintended for me
Living simply

In summers
I got the chance to experience the slow lane
Wandering about at my family's homestead
In rural Michigan
Nothing to do
But enjoy whatever showed up each day
No phones
No computers
No car
Playing games with eight siblings and
Cousins sharing one bike

Yet

Much of the year
I felt "on call" to overloaded parents and others
Who expected me to say yes to all requests
Saying no was not an option
My space stolen by others
Not recognizing my need

My mother created space for herself
When she meditated one hour each day
My father had his space of grace
Through fasting, prayer, and Bible study
I need space for God, people, places, and things of
my life

Nature offers lessons about space
Plants need their space to grow and stretch toward light
The sea reigns in its own space through tides of change
The sun, moon, and stars have their spaces
Why can't I?

The answer comes to me
Loud and clear
I am the CEO of my own life
For me
Space is in the slow lane
I choose or not
What spaces I need

Space to listen from within
Space to be with family and friends
Space to speak or not
Space to fall down and get up again
Space to rescue that orphan plant
Offering it water and a place to grow again
Space to hear and receive voices of hope
Space to watch the morning unfold
Space to say goodnight to the sunset

Space to sing, laugh, work, pray and play
Space to just be with me
Space for gratitude for everything

Yes

Space in the slow lane is what's for me
Filled with gems-
     love, peace,
     faith, patience,
     acceptance, compassion,
     kindness, and light

Space

A gift I give to me
Every day!

In the House of Regret

Sorrow lives there
In the bedroom
Expectations and disappointments await
Assumptions claim the living room
Impatience in an adjourning room
Shame
Self-accusation
Guilt
Lament
Hang in the closet
The kitchen filled with
Remorse, misinformation, and misunderstanding
While in the bathroom
Pictures of the past adorn the walls
I walk into this smothering, dark house and soon say
Goodbye
Next door
I enter an abode of delight
Where bright light resides
Courage
Hope
Contentment
Meet me at the door
My soul is satisfied in this
New place of love!

Conversation with Myself

I reached out to care for others
Not mindful of caring for myself
Waiting for others
To give me unconditional love
Waiting for others to hear me beyond the fog of chatter
Waiting to see myself
As if I matter

The wait is over
Now I know what to do

Give myself unconditional love
Listen to myself as my angelic guide
See myself as God sees me
Touch myself with loving kindness
Embrace all of me
My body, mind, emotions, spirit, relationships ...
Realize that my thoughts, words, and deeds matter to me
and to the world
Examine the source of my values
Decide to let go of what no longer works for me

As I learn on this journey called life
I want to be
Unafraid and courageous
Not because of the permission from others
But by the God given freedom to just be

For I am a part of the wholeness of life
In a dance of coexistence

Like that succulent plant on the side of the path
Reaching for the light
As do I

Like that baby seal decomposing on the beach
Answering its final call on planet earth
So will I
Someday

The Pacific Ocean can be only what it is
Not the shimmering bay waters
Glistening like diamonds in bright light
Nor
Azure blue Lake Michigan touching shores in evening light
Nor
A river, creek, estuary, delta, canal, bayou
Each
Beautiful and unique
But not the sea

Message clear
Be me
Give me to me
A loving gift to myself
Discover my inner being
Explore diversity all around

Loving myself is a blessing to the world
It's easy to love others
When I love ME!

Fall into Love

When you wake up
in the morning
As sad as could be
Fall into love
To inspire thee

When clouds abound
Everywhere you turn
Fall into love
To lift you up

When you don't know where to go
Nor
What to do
Fall into love
It's always there to guide you

When you can't see your way clear
From your world view
Fall into love
To light the way through

When friends come and go
Like waves of the sea
Fall into love and
Carry on with ease

When you can't see light
In darkest night
Fall into love
To be there with you

When chaos reigns
Fall into love
To receive the fresh grace of peace

Where is that love
You ask?
Gaze into your heart
It's right there
For you
Always!

Linger There

When shroud of darkness
Invades your day
Linger in the space of hope

When problems of life
Shower down like thunderous rain
Linger in the space of hope

When light is hidden
From dawn to dusk
Linger in the space of hope

When questions sans answers
Create dissonance of spirit
Linger in the space of hope

When all else fails
Remember
This, too, shall pass
Invite love to join you
As you linger

In the space of hope

Self-Discovery

Shroud of sadness
Murky as thick gray billows
Hovered over my dreams
Hijacking my sleep

What called forth this unconscious misery?

Oh yes
Now I remember yesterday
Encountering assumptions of care
Not offered nor given
Drunkened by the wine of flattery
Enticed to a place I really didn't want to be
Rather than promptly speaking up
I walked on the road called forgetfulness
Stopping along the way to sip the nectar of false pride
Unaware of the present moment

The light of morning
Helped me to see with new eyes
The gateway to self-respect

Knowing myself is the key
Setting me free to say what I
Truly feel and what really
Works for me
Choosing
Moment by moment
To give and receive love
As the way to be

Perfect Trust

I wonder if those raindrops have perfect trust in gravity
Or
Will doubt keep them suspended between heaven and
Earth?

What of those vibrant yellow flowers in the meadow there
Do they have perfect trust that sunlight will find them?

As I journey today
Do I have perfect trust in divine guidance?

Yes!
Yes!
Yes!

What does perfect trust look like?
It's a baby's smile
In the safety of the mother's arms

It's that monarch butterfly
On wings of hope trusting in the process of
Seeking and finding a mate
To continue the species
Then surrendering to its final fate

It's that chirping bird calling into the wind
It is the waves of the sea roaring to shore
Becoming one with the tides

When I awake
I rise with perfect trust in the goodness of life

When death has had its say
And my body says goodbye to planet earth
I have perfect trust in
Forever!

The Honey in a Jar

That honey
Raw
Unfiltered
White
Hidden out of sight for months

Not sure if it was spoiled or not
I was willing to let it go
But it lingered on for days
There
At the bottom of the jar beneath tepid water
Not yet ready to go down the drain
Into the unknown

Such a reminder of life
Sometimes
I am of a mind to let go of stuff
Other times
Not
When fear whispers
"Don't let go"
"Don't let go"
I hold on to thoughts, feelings, things
No longer needed or desired
At times
I am
Just like that honey
Not yet wanting to embrace
That sweet, enticing surrender
To change!

Step into Your Peace

When you wake up in the morning
From a restless night of sleep
Rise
Be still
Look for the light within and
Step into your peace

When you wonder what to do
In the fog of discordant thoughts
Be still
Look for the light within and
Step into your peace

When you can't find forgotten stuff right in front of you
Let go and
Step into your peace

When busyness gets in the way
Sit for a while and pray
Then
Step into your peace

When neighborhood noise disrupts
Dismiss it with a song in your heart and
Step into your peace

When all is said and done
And you can't seem to find quietude
Knock on the door of love
Step right in
Receive
Your gift of peace!

Exclusion/Inclusion

In early morn
Four construction workers
Gather in a circle before work
Their communal gathering
Brought to my mind
The question
What does it feel like to be the outsider?

Society has lots of ways of excluding others
Racism, sexism, homophobia,
Cultural norms, traditions, tribal and religious customs
Can be vehicles of exclusion
So alien to nature's way

The sun, moon, and stars don't exclude plants or animals
As they light the world
Air doesn't exclude people on one side of town
Nor the other
Raindrops fall on everything as they land on the earth

Inclusion is the way to celebrate our shared existence
Offering gifts of friendship, creativity
Compassion, respect, and kindness
Exclusionary behavior isolates, separates, divides
Perpetuating illusions of elitism
Less than and greater than

Love

The great equalizer
Includes all
in the circle of life

I found this out as I experienced
Love of myself
Love of nature
The loving kindness of family, friends, strangers

Matters not the structures of exclusion in the world
I cannot be excluded
For I am loved by divine grace

And so are you!

Ageless Grace

When cares of life beckon despair

Keep moving

When fog of gloom hijacks your joy

Keep stepping

When fear overtakes hope

Be still

When sadness fills your heart

Look for the light

When days and nights seem the same

Trust that divine love

Will carry you through it all

This I Believe

I believe that the sun is shining
Even when I don't see it

I believe that waves of the sea change
With the waxing and waning of the moon

I believe that flowers will bloom in their season
I believe that walking in nature heals me

I believe that caring for my holy body temple
Is my commitment to wellness

I believe that my mind takes in my environment through my
Senses affecting what I think, how I feel, and what I do
Thus, I must choose carefully what enters my inner space

I believe that we are all connected through omnipresent
Love

I believe that the more I get to know my authentic self
The more I am able to give and receive love

I believe that imagination ignites creativity

I believe that I am responsible for my life
Paying attention
My daily practice

I believe that my beliefs influence my behavior

I believe that all things in this temporary world will change

I believe that each day is new and will never be again

Territory

In early morn
The light shines through two holes of dense haze
Like giant cat eyes watching the world go by
These sky features
Beckon memories of cats in the wild

Lions, tigers, leopards, cheetahs ...
Must know their territory for survival
What food and water are available?
Where are the trespassers?
Where to safely protect newborns
Some are solo travelers
Others live in communities
No doubt about it
One careless mistake could be their fatal fate

Birds, bees, plants have their territories
Earthlings, too
We call them
Cities, states, nations, provinces, empires, colonies, nations,
Neighborhoods, farms ...

Alas
Over centuries until now
People have fought wars over territories
Boldly stealing gold, silver, people
Without apology
Genocide, murder, destruction of many kinds
Used as weapons of mass destruction

Societies have ways to define, confine, control, unite and
Separate territories
With countless boundaries and borders across the globe

Yet
Beyond the physical plane
Is the aura of spirit in everything
Invisible to the naked eye

I look at Mona Lisa's smile to see her intriguing beauty
I feel the sensuous nature of Georgia O'Keeffe's paintings
Her splendid vision of gigantic flowers awakens my heart
I listen to music that makes me want to dance

What is this of which I speak
Beyond tangible territory?
It's omnipresent Spirit of love
Free to all!

Faith Journey

In the chill of early morn
Milky white bay waters
Reflect hazy sky
Red hue over there
Heralds fresh sunrise
Not yet seen over yonder hills

Along highway
Drooping leaves of tall trees
Await warmth
To lift their arms into light
In praise of this holy day

Soon

Luminous glow reveals waves of white clouds
Etched on blue canvas
Unlike white-capped sea waves
Dancing to another rhythm
On and on they go
As do we

Journeying
To unknown destinies
Free as could be

It's Personal

When will I forgive myself
For trespassing against my body?
Not honoring the precious gift of territory
The space where my spirit, mind, emotions reside?

When will I understand that I am more than
muscles, bones, cells, blood, tissue, fascia
But a complexity of interdependent, interactive, dynamic
Elements in never ending circles of change
In need of rest, nourishment, movement, care

When will I stop allowing mindlessness
And impulsive behavior to yank my body out of tranquility?

When will I learn to be fully present in my body as I move
About in the world?

Spirit echoes
There is a way

Be intentional
Listen to the quiet voice of wisdom
Connect to your spirit animating your body
To be the best that it can be

I need my body to express my divinity
As a precious jewel
Shining
With the glory of love
In every breath

In My Name

Wars, mayhem, deceit
Theft of lands, nations, people, resources
In my name

Immigrant children caged liked animals
Prisoners held without bond for petty crimes
In my name

Misuse of public resources for the all mighty dollar
By corporate greed
In my name

Rape of landscape
Here and there
In my name

Pollution of air, sea, space
In my name

Fear mongering, lies, corruption
Relentless retreat from truth
Whenever
However
Wherever
In my name

Public policies, rules, regulations
Defining use of public space
Created and approved by local, state, and federal
Policymakers known as politicians
Judges and the U.S. President, too
In my name

Yes

There are actions by governments at all levels
That assault our inalienable Rights of life, liberty, and the
Pursuit of happiness
As declared in the U.S. Declaration of Independence

Deeds in America and around the world
In our collective name
"We," the people

Some people have found ways to say
No!
Not in my name

Quakers said **No!** to slave laws
In covert and overt ways
Not in my name

Harriet Tubman said
No!
Not in my name

Putting on her traveling shoes
Following the north star
Walking from bondage to freedom
With determination, hope, and a rifle

James Baldwin, Toni Morrison, Alice Walker
Eleanor Roosevelt and many more
Exclaiming their prophetic truths
No!
Not in my name

Advocates of all stripes
Working for social justice, protecting the environment
And legions of issues for the good of humankind say
No!
Not in my name

We, the people, say
Yes!

In our name
Justice

In our name
Compassion

In our name
Kindness

In our name
Respect for all life

In our name
Owning the consequences
Of our individual and collective actions

In our name
Love for all!

Absent

It was a gift
The perfect fit
Sleek, slim, my favorite color blue
I reached for it this morning

OMG
Panic crept in when I couldn't find it
Where could it be?
When did I last have it?

An uneasy pause
Didn't calm my fears
The thought of the loss
Would not let me go
Like a bulldog holding on in a street fight

I finally accepted the fact
It would not to be found
At least not now

I realized
I had mindlessly misplaced my favorite ballpoint pen
It was in my house or not

What did I learn from my unresolved loss?
Let go of being absent from NOW

Morning News

Sun
Shining amid gray clouds
Reflects a giant footprint
On smooth bay waters
They
Coexist in shared space

Swimmers
Fishermen
Walkers
Cyclists
Runners
A woman howling on the beach
Share public space

Sea creatures
Coexist with each other and the sea
Wildebeests on African plains
Coexist with lions
Humans
Coexist in families, tribes, communities, nations

What about me?
How do I coexist inside myself
With my many thoughts, feelings, body parts
Circling round and round
In endless dynamics of change

I hear the message of the morn
Love all of me
With total acceptance, kindness, gentleness
Listening with an open heart
Feeling with compassion
Those parts of me still waiting for healing
Awake to life
In plain sight

Love the moment
It will love you back

Tribute to My Mother: Truesillia Bryson Lenox*

Although my mother has been gone
From this physical plane since 1982
My habits of this morning
Reminded me that she is alive and well
In my memories, thoughts, and feelings

She
At age 24
Married a widower with three children
Ages 12, 11, 6

He
Ambitious
Focused
Determined to make a life in the alien City of Chicago
On their honeymoon

Both
Almost killed in an automobile accident during a
Snowstorm
Never treated in a hospital
Because....

Still
They carried on
Having six more children (one deceased as an infant)

By the time I was born
Mother was 34
I imagine
Already fatigued from caring for five children and endless
Service to church and community
Two siblings came after my birth

She
Matriarch of the family
Answering the needs, wants, desires, and expectations of
Nine people
Her eight children and her husband
Each demanding attention in their own unique ways

She
Always responding with kindness and love

But "What about her?" I ask
She found a way to nurture her soul
Staying connected to the Spirit of God
Through daily meditation, reading the Bible, and listening to
Moody Bible Institute Radio all day
When we traveled as a family to our summer home in rural
Michigan

She had a last minute routine of "double checking" the stove
(Which I did this morning)
Making sure the gas was off, checking doors
Looking around for forgotten items
All the while
Interacting with her children in their drama of the moment

Mother's agenda for her children was to educate them
She intentionally established a firm spiritual foundation
For our lives
We had after-school Bible study at the home of a neighbor
Sunday school and a myriad of other church activities

She
A woman of deep sorrow
Never overcame the loss of her mother
At age 14
Homeless
Sent to homes of relatives
Finally given shelter
In the home of an older woman
Until she married my father

As a child
I saw her struggles
I felt her pain
I knew not what to do
I did what I was asked
Hoping it would lift her spirits
And ease her fears

It wasn't enough
I finally got that
I couldn't take her burdens away

That sense of helplessness
Made me sad
I now understand that each of us is on our own journey
With joys, sorrows, and lessons to learn

As I look back through the lens of maturity
I am seeing my mother with eyes of compassion and love
Her love of God and family
Her strength and determination
Her faith and hope
Her kindness and generosity
All
Enriching my life today

She struggled and survived Until age 69
When she said
"Let me go, I want to go to my heavenly home.
I'm done!"
Thank you, dear mother
Thank you!

*Wife of Bishop Eleazar Lenox

Relationships

A Rare Gift

A friend gazes into your heart
With unconditional love
Listening with compassion
To words spoken and unsaid
Disclosing secrets in sphere of mutual trust and respect
Sharing, caring, daring
Holding space of hope for
Dreams, wants, desires
Quick to forgive and return again
To where it all began
Simple pleasures become treasures
With smiles that delight
Tenderly
Refining each other
Like iron sharpens iron
In an invisible bond
Of giving and receiving
Season after season
Walking in the light of kindness
Kindred spirits
Like waves of the sea
Separate yet together
On this journey
Called life

In the Presence of Greatness

What can I say about being in the presence of a great poet?
Hearing her words breathe into my soul with a refreshing
Innocence
Humble and bold

Her kind and gentle spirit
Touching my heart with her holy light
Quietly speaking the voices of ex-slaves who gave life and
Limb
For a war that excluded them from pensions for service
Rendered for a nation unwilling to acknowledge them

She offered a glimpse of what love looks like when she told
Of a church sister
Who gave unconditional love to everyone that sacred night

What can I say about an evening with U.S. Poet Laureate
Tracy K. Smith?
Warm as a mother's joy
Gracious as a queen
Her happy smile
Welcoming one and all into her landscape of dreams and
Reality

It is no mystery that Tracy K. Smith is a brilliant intellect
Awakening the world through poetry
To the realness of life

Yet
With a tenderness
Born of love

What can I say about Tracy K. Smith?
Who inspires, informs, and delights
With the fragrance of truth

Showing us how to embrace hope
In desperate times
Challenging us
To remember our forgotten stories
Her guidance
Encouraging us to be the best that we can be
With freedom to listen and learn
From each other

My heart overflows with joy
For the privilege of beholding her greatness
The greatness of spirit
The greatness of compassion
The greatness of an exquisite wordsmith
The greatness of a prophetic vision
The greatness of service
Baptizing us with poetry
Healing our hearts as we see new light
Thank you
Tracy K. Smith!

Being

Profound changes in the atmosphere of life require
Patience
    Persistence
        Passion
            Perseverance
            Power
                To live in the moment

Breath of God

Oh
To feel the breath of God
Like those trees along the side of the road
Holding on to the light
Inhaling the freshness of morning

Oh
To feel the breath of God
In the stillness of bay waters
Reflecting blue skies

Oh
To feel the breath of God
Hearing the mighty sea
Echoing its sounds of praise in every wave

Oh
To feel the breath of God
As effortlessly as that egret
Flying in space

Oh
To say yes to the breath of God
With gratitude in my heart

Journey Within

In my innermost being
Silence
Welcomes me home
No luggage or companions needed
In this space of solitude
Just an open heart and wakeful awareness
My soul invites me to stay a while
Receiving eternal love
Breath by breath

Of Kindness

I awakened in early morn
My body thankful
For the gift of patience
To be as slow as I wanted to be

Soon

Memories of the sea
Beckoned me to go and see the wondrous one
I strolled on the path
Hearing its loud roar
Like a rushing freight train
Before I saw my muse
There
At low tide

Onward I walked on the sands
Wondering if the seaweed on the beach
Would ride the waters again
Walking toward home
I saw a written message on a fence
"Be kind"

Kindness grows with
Tenderness, patience, service

Kindness is a way of love
Lifting spirits
One by one
What would this world be without kindness?

Delicious Memories

At horizon of early morn
Soothing sweet peach hue
Beckons memories
Of leisure summer days in Michigan
Eating fresh-picked greens
Peach cobblers, and delectable choices
From abundant vegetable garden
Cooked with love by an elder named Mother Brown and
My mother's sister, Lorene

Playing made up games with siblings and cousins
Mother and aunt singing, praying, and sharing stories
Whispering secrets while doing chores
No worries in this rural haven of rest
Just fellowship, kinship, and peace

Unlike Chicago dwelling
Filled with complexities
Relentless noise
Obscene wealth of few
Amid poverty of most
Racial and class divides
And numerous other realities
Of the urban jungle

Absent father committed to
Leading saints to heavenly gates
Little time for family was his fate

My parents gave the gift of
Shielding their children from ghetto ways
Late June until Labor Day each year
To dwell a while in open spaces
Living the simple life

There
I first saw the light of God
In the jewels of nature
Awakening my heart with joy

I remember
With a smile
Those glorious times
The source of love
That keep on giving

Lindsay

Murky gray haze
Shrouds the sky
Like thick sadness in my heart
Witnessing the struggles of my dear friend
Enduring the rages of cancer
How can this be?
She:
So brilliant
So young
So vibrant
So creative
So loving
So kind
So gracious
So courageous
God knows! I don't!
Yet
I know this:
We live on planet earth marked by nanoseconds, days,
Months, years
To the end of existence in this temporary world
Gastrotrichs live for 3 days
Birds join the parade for a few years
Four generations of migrating butterflies live, mate and die
Before reaching their place in a warmer climate
Thence to begin a new
Flowers, trees, and more
Bow to the inevitable
Leaving seeds for next generations

Rummel Pinera's shortest poem
"Go
Cry!
Bye"
Says much about the brevity of things
Whatever the time
Long or short
We breathe the breath of life
Until
At last
Say goodbye to earth matters as we
Journey into the eternity of light
Unencumbered
Praise God for omnipresent love
Always with us
To carry us onward

See Me!

I saw her approaching the boardwalk
An orange bandana covering all but her eyes
Then I heard her words
"Thank you" as I picked up trash to put in the nearby barrel

The debris
Dropped
With effortless ease into the waste container

I said to her
"Look at that mighty sea"

She

Old
In tattered clothing
Maybe homeless
Maybe not
Pulled down her bandana to answer me
Revealing lots of missing teeth
Our conversation continued

Each time she finished speaking
She placed the bandana back over much of her face
Maybe ashamed of her mouth
Maybe not

Yet her joyous, animated voice
Celebrated our shared appreciation and mutual
Understanding
Her gentle eyes beamed with delight

As we talked about the source and gifts of the sea
Eventually
We said goodbye

I

Ever grateful for the lesson
To look beyond appearance
To give and receive love
Heart to heart

She

No longer a stranger
But a kindred soul
Connected by divine Spirit

Who Are They?

Who are they?
Who hide their self-loathing
Behind a curtain of darkness
All the while
Spouting venomous words
To intimidate others
So like a poisonous snake
Defending itself

Who are they?
Who feel no shame
With mean deeds
And hateful games
On social media
And other ways

Who are they?
Who think and say
I am better than you
I want you to feel smaller/less valuable than me

Who are they?
Who hold deceit
In a web of false beliefs
Feeling powerless
Yet
All the while
Attacking others
With lies and treachery

Who are they?
Whose
Anger
Fear
Revengefulness
Harm others
With aggressive, intimidating tactics

Who are they?
Who infuse the atmosphere
With a blizzard of hatred
For lack of knowledge
Of another way

Who are they?
Who do not understand
That each and every person
On the planet
Is a unique expression of
The glory of diversity

Who are they?
Who refuse to see
We are all connected
Brothers
Sisters
ALL

We are
One giant global family
On earth
Look in the mirror
What do you see?
Do you see a bully
Looking straight at thee?
Do you feel
Helpless
Hopeless
Defeated
Really wanting to say
"Help me, help me
"For I know
No other way"

The answer
Is right there
Inside of you
Your lovely, unique self
Awaits you

Look around
See that WE are connected
Near and far
By our shared humanity

Respect yourself
By word and deed
Others will reciprocate
Indeed

You can decide
From this day forward
I will let my light shine
Regardless

Oh
How happy
You will be
To feel the joy
Of *that* discovery

So
Before acting
In unkind ways
Stop!
Think!
Feel!
Ask!
Do I want to receive
What I am giving out
Today?

Mindful

Do I see? or do I just look?

Do I listen? or do I just hear?

Do I savor the experience?

Or do I flee the moment?

Do I see the face of God in me

Like I see it in you?

The Old Man and His Dog

There they were
At the beach
An elderly gentleman and his dog, barely able to move
Waiting with the patience of Job

The dog
With numerous straps to protect his torso
Breathing deeply
Standing still
Trying to decide when to take the next step

The old man waiting calmly
Until the dog slowly took one step
Then
After what seemed like a very long time
Took another step
Stopping
Before starting again
Walking at a snail's pace

I left
Grateful that I noticed
Man and dog
Each
In a dance of acceptance and tolerance
Surrendering to the aging process

Why?

"Why are you here?"
The old white man in front of me asked
As I stood in line to get lunch
At an exclusive yacht club in San Diego
As the only person of color in the room except for an
Elderly male waiter
I was stunned speechless by the question

I soon recovered enough to answer
"To hear the lecture"
He made no response
Later reflecting on his question and my response
I wished that I had replied to him
"Why are YOU here?"

His annoying, rude, inquisition
Brought to my mind
Dissonant thoughts and utter amazement
For such a question to be asked of me
In 2019!

Later
I looked beyond that question to a larger context
"Why am I here on planet earth?"
That is a question for me to ask myself
 Similar to the theological question
"What is my purpose here in this world?"

The answer goes beyond matters of work, play,
Possessions, knowledge
The reply sprung from my innermost being
I am here to love
Freely given and received by God's grace

Nature

In Praise of Color

Color
The divine gift that decorates life
Ever present in plain sight

Red, purple, orange, pink
Announcing sunrises and sunsets

Green grasses, plants, and trees
Radiate their refreshing glow of tranquility
The colors of a rainbow inspire dreams

Color
Rings the bells of emotions
Fiery red may echo anger
The soothing blue of sky and sea
Blissful yellow brightens the heart

Vibrating colors of the seven chakras of the body
Emit the life force through energetic channels
Symbolic colors abound in countless religions and cultures

Color
Endless possibilities
But
Color can't exist without the presence of light
I can't imagine life without it
What colors will be with me on my spiritual journey?
Will it be the colors of peace, love, wisdom, tranquility
Reflected by divine light from within?

Oh
May it be so!

Ode to the Sweet Potato

Oh
Sweet, sweet potato
How splendid *you are*
With copper coat and lush orange flesh
Calling forth memories of the *sun* in autumn dawn
Rising into a clear *blue sky*

Your bark-like skin
With lumps and bumps
So reminiscent of life
Holding memories of forgotten experiences

Your singular color
In vivid boldness
Hidden within
Like circular waves in a pond
Or
The sun amid a constellation of planets afar

But you are so much more
Your secret divinity
Discovered by Aunt Honey, Aunt Hortense, Aunt Violet,
Aunt Jessie
And many other ancestors long gone
Sliced, diced, baked, boiled, and fried your roots
Transforming your deliciousness
Into mouthwatering sweet potato pies, candied yams,
Mashed potatoes

Oh
How they knew you
From the inside out
Beautifying plates with sumptuousness and yummy tastes

Like all of us
You need your own unique space
Growing from roots to tubers
In your cocoon of warm darkness
While your vine green leaves above ground
Packed with nutrients
Reach toward light

After leaving your birth chamber
You ripen into sweetness
Like an old friend
Your sacrifice for others cannot be forgotten
For every time your goodness enters within
It's like an exquisite gift

Yes
There are Yukon Golds, Saxons, and other spuds
But you are the queen with your richness
Of vitamins, minerals, fiber, estrogen, and soothing texture
So versatile and true
Authentically you!

Imagine

Before the beginning of time
Before life as we know it began
Before heaven, earth, or the moon
Before trilobites, eurypterids, or dinosaurs
Before Neanderthals or homo sapiens came to be
Before continents or nations formed
Before microorganisms, genes, bacteria, DNA, or RNA
Before coming and going of ice ages
Before humans came to be
Before tools, civilizations, or cultural diversity emerged
    from human ingenuity
Before apes, chimpanzees, lions, zebras, elephants
Before sea creatures great and small
Before trees, flowers, silver, coal or gold
Before agriculture changed the planet
Before Shango, Vishnu, Zeus, Sedna, Ra, Isis, Tudi Gong
Pharaohs, pyramids, dynasties, or empires existed
Before Jesus walked the earth or Buddha found truth
Before Sanskrit or dead sea scrolls
Before industrialization revolutionized the world
Before nanoseconds, internet, iPad, phones, networks, or
Global communication
Before clouds, chocolate, or calendars
Before you or I existed
There was the sun
Offering glorious light and hope
Then and now
Imagine
What the sun has seen
In its 4.6 billion years of life!

Singularity of Purpose

In dark night and scant light of morn
Raindrops descend to earth with living waters
Nourishing fauna, flora, earthlings

Separate
Yet
Together
Answering the call of destiny
With singularity of purpose

What if we could be like raindrops
Showering the earth with love
Wherever we are
With a song of peace!

Seeing

There it was
Just above yonder hill
A feathery cloud pausing in space
As if sketched by God on a canvas of blue
Luminous glow enfolds land and sea while
Peachy hue announces
Apollo's gift
Chirping birds
Echo morning call
New life revealed
As far as you can see

A Walk by the Sea

The smell of the sea
Evokes memories of salt and fish

I hear the sea
Roaring like tumultuous rain on a stormy night

I trust the sea for the air I breathe

I notice those sandpipers with thin long beaks
Seeking and finding morsels to eat
Taking what is needed and no more

I see pelicans soaring high above
Peaceful as a summer dream
No doubts
No fears
Just pure trust in the universe

What would the world be like
If we awaken to the abundance of creation
Void of greed and separation with space for all?

I smile as I remember my friend's words:
"God has grace for us all."
"All that God has is for us all."

Day into Night

Gray haze at dawn
Eclipses sky
    Raindrops
        Come and go
           Sleepy light
               Invites an afternoon nap
                  Meadow greens
                    Refreshed by wetness
                    Smile with delight
                    Calm day leans
                      Seamlessly
                        Into dusk
                    Night claims atmosphere
                      Saturated with *rain*

Gaze of the Sun

I wonder
What does the sun see through the veil of clouds?
Does it see the trembling bay waters flowing to shore
And the capsized boat on the beach?
Does it hear the sounds of the crows and Mourning Doves
Claiming their territory in the neighborhood?
Does it see those birds-of-paradise, red begonias, and royal
Purple bougainvilleas reaching for its light?
Does it hear the silent prayers of the lady facing the sea as
White-capped waves roar toward her relentlessly?
What of the full moon revolving around the globe this day
And mountaintops
Welcoming the presence of God
Does it see those, too?
I wonder
Does it see me walking along the seaward path hoping for
A touch of inspiration?
Does it see my heart dance with glee
As I awaken to its hug of love?
I wonder

In Clarity of Light

Dawn fades into bright morn
Crows call
"Come out into the mystery"
Risen sun
Hugs land and sea
In luminous clarity of new beginning
Pristine blue sky
Excites my heart with joy
Smiling with thankfulness
For gifts
Wrapped in the blessing of NOW!

New Dawning

Brilliant sun rises in clear blue skies
Birds
Navigate uncertainties in flights of hope
She walks along boardwalk
Whispering a prayer of praise
Listening to the rhythms of the sea
Singing song of change
Sandy beach
Freshly groomed by workmen
Appears as ribbons of silent waves
Waiting for whatever will be
Omnipresent light
Offers unconditional love
Free
To everyone!

Illusion and Reality

In early morn
Residential buildings on opposite side of bay
Reflects on bay waters

The scene brings to mind
Memories of New York skyscrapers
Standing side by side
In early morning light

The illusion
Changes with the light
Eventually disappearing as sunlight
Breaks through gray clouds

What was this magical moment saying to me?
Light changes everything
Illuminating what is real and not
The bay is real
Yet the reflection of the buildings
On the water
Seemed as an illusion
Enhanced by my imagination

Would I have thought the same of what I saw
If I had not seen New York City's iconic buildings?

I think not

Illusions are in the eye of the beholder
Enriched by perception, experience, imagination
So, too, creation
From imagination to real

Edison imagined the possibility of a light bulb
Working with scientists until they created that marvel of
Electric light

Henry Ford's vision, persistence, and determination
To "put America on wheels"
Transformed the nation from an agrarian to an
Industrial society

Lindbergh fulfilled his dream of a solo flight across the
Atlantic that became the basis of aviation as we know it
Today

Imagination, practice, trial and error
And
Leaps of faith inspire creation in our world

The light of truth
Tells us what is real and what is not

Transformation

There it was on the kitchen counter
Pear-shaped
It's inner sanctum
Of lime hue edged by dark green
A huge seed resting in its perfect crater

The fruit
Ripe and ready for a voyage
First enjoyed by my eyes
Then
Diced into small pieces
Placed on brown bread toast
Moist, buttery and rich with flavor
I ate it too fast

Yet
Wanting it to last
Isn't that what impatience is all about?
Hurrying up to get and keep what won't last
Holding on to the illusion
That fast is the way

The green miracle with black skin
Transformed by my digestive system
Gave me nutrients for my eyes, liver,
Skin, digestion, blood glucose,
Bones and more

What an amazing blessing this morn
A magical Hass avocado
Reborn in me!

New Beginning

Bright star of morn
Near
Yet so far
Thank you for coming once again
To anoint my heart with joy
Warming my body, mind, and spirit
As only you can do

Oh
How glad I am
That you are here
For the earth is void
Without your touch
So dear

The Sunflowers

In bright sun
A pot of brilliant sunflowers
Reached for me as I passed by
Echoing
"Take me home with you"

My visit to the greenhouse was not to buy that plant
But I did!
Its happy yellow blooms made me smile

The next morning
A few petals were drooping like the skin of an old woman
With edges of white death appearing beneath the yellow hue
Sadness zapped my heart
As I realized the inevitable

Then I noticed
Hidden beneath the adults
Tiny buds wrapped tightly in green leaves
Offered hope for new blossoms
To brighten my
"Someday"

Beingness

Gentle winds
Touching Dawn
Just being, just being

Delicate flowers
Along narrow path
Just being, just being

Birds-of-paradise
Over there
Just being, just being

Chirping birds
Singing call to friends
Just being, just being

Roaring ocean
Gray as sky
Just being, just being

Canopy of old tree branches
Holding secrets etched
In strips of brokenness
Just being, just being

I walk along the seashore
Just being, just being

Do I Hear Rain?

Do I hear rain?
Making an offering
To the gods of the sea?

Do I hear rain?
That miracle of life
Infusing all of life

Do I hear rain?
That awesome wetness
Visiting rivers, streams, brooks, seas
And all in between

Do I hear rain?
Those droplets like pearls,
Downpours, and more
Dazzling heaven and earth

Do I hear rain?
Replenishing lakes
Great and small
With fresh water

Do I hear rain?
Sounding like a symphony of serenity
Like Jessye Norman singing
Ava Maria

Do I hear rain?
Summoning memories
Of that precious day of traveling through

The richness of rain
From drizzle to thunderstorms
And mist, too
Soothing my spirit with
Heavenly bliss

Do I hear rain?
Pausing
Now and then
More or less
On seven continents:
Africa, Asia, Europe
North America
South America
Antarctica
Australia

Do I hear rain?
Giver of life
And sometimes death
Continuing onward
Through clouds of change

Do I hear rain?
That essential element of life
Like love
That we all need

Thank you, dear rain
Thank you!

I Wonder

How do plants know what to do to survive?
How do they know their own kind?
How do they know to reach for the light to thrive?

What of the butterfly
How does it know it's role in the chain of life?
Scientists, philosophers, psychologists, ethnologists...
Seek to understand the secret lives of plants and animals
Some argue that they have consciousness
What are the similarities and differences of consciousness
Of humankind from other forms of life?
I do not know the answer to these questions

But
This I do know

Light is the source of energy for all life
Without the light of the sun and the heat it provides
Life on earth would not exist

Somehow
Animals, plants, people
Have ways of knowing how
To seek and find the light
That eternal life-force
Connecting us
In the oneness of all life

The Sun

When will I see the sun?
That orb
Bringing light for our days

When will I see the sun?
That ancient miracle
Birthed before mountains, animals, trees, humans

When will I see the sun?
Hot, intense like a Mississippi July

When will I see the sun?
That yellow glow
Dazzling my spirit with inspiration

When will I see the sun?
Warming me like a cloudless summer day in San Diego

Dim light
Tells me it is there
Beyond the milky white haze
Smiling at me
As the earth rotates
Round and round

The magnificent presence of the sun
A marvelous wonder!

Good Morning Sunday

At the horizon

Black lake

Meets blue green gold orange

Day emerging

In clear sky

Sunrise

Not yet seen

Atmosphere assaulted by sounds of motorists

Rushing through the quiet calm

Of first light

Only a Look

There
Leaning over the guard rail adjacent to the highway
Looking into freedom land
That lush valley below of
Disparate green shrubs, trees, flowers
Perfectly still
Receiving moisture from a thin veil of fog
She
Had the wisdom to stop and pause
Silently taking in the beauty below
As cars roared by
She
Seemingly
Unperturbed by rush hour traffic
The serenity of twilight
Long gone
Replaced with urban noise
Yet
She could have been me
Enjoying the peace of the moment
Looking at the natural world
Taking a sip of the nectar of joy
Right there on the side of road
My heart smiled with happiness
As I continued on my journey
Remembering
To savor the blessings

The Sparrow

The lone sparrow
Jumped into my view
So confidently landing on the nearby shrub
Chirping as if it owned the world
Then taking off into the mystery

Was it a house sparrow
Or one of 25 other species in its family?
Living among us in agricultural terrains, cities, caves,
Ancient places for more than 10,000 years
Their recent disappearance in London

Puzzling

Why did they leave?
Where did they go?
Some suggest their primary food, insects, especially
Needed for their newborns
Are diminishing in the city
No one knows why
This most common, widespread, adaptable bird on earth
Missing in London, England

Eaten as a delicacy
Killed by the millions in China to protect rice fields
Hunted and murdered for sporting games

Talked about in biblical texts and secular literature
The subject of painters from the East and West

The sparrow
Reminds me of what it does best

Survive

No matter what

And so do
You and I!

Seaweed

Seaweed oh seaweed
Where have you been?
How long have you traveled to arrive at Mission Beach?
Will this be your final home or be taken away to the landfill?
Perhaps you will dance yet again
With your romance with the sea

Do you see that father and daughter sitting there?
She
Discovering gravity
Tossing sand into the air

Seaweed oh seaweed
When and where were you born?
What have you seen
In your travels?

Unlike that Torrey Pine Tree
Growing in place by the bay
You seem to dwell on rocky shores
And tidal pools in hues of red, green, brown
In need of light to grow
Just like me

Seaweed oh seaweed
What say you to me this morn

Be at home
Here and now
As am I
There is a place for you
Wherever you are
Sunny skies or not

Potpourri

Potpourri

Allness

Journeys of life are as distinct as the stars
So many encounters along the way
Each
A part of the whole

What do I carry on my journey?
Spirit answers:
Become friends with God
Get to know your authentic self
Find your truth in stillness
Practice patience
Trust the flow of change
Listen to Spirit
Be thankful for everything
Make no assumptions
Attend to your intentions
Live with an open heart
Rise
Claim the eternity of
Now!

Morning Gifts on St. Patrick's Day

I walked on a path toward the bay
Suddenly
I heard an unfamiliar flutter
High up among the green leaves of a palm tree
There
A male parrot
Dressed in rich pastel green
Flying with blackbirds
Peacefully sharing the neighborhood space

The surprise encounter
Caused me to pause and really look
At the nearby giant forest green tropical tree
Reaching for light

A corridor of diverse green succulents
In brilliant sunlight
Welcomed me as I strolled toward the beach

Blossoms of some flowers
Remain closed in chilly air
Soon
The warmth of the sun anointed their petals
As they opened their faces toward light

Seaside
White capped waves with a hint of green
Rush to shore with relentless persistence
Leaving behind
Mounds of light green, brown, and red seaweed
On the beach

Green
The color of growth, harmony, freshness, fertility
Green
The color of nature
Green
The symbol of ever refreshing life
Green
A gift of healing in plain sight

Praise be this day of celebration
Honoring the ancient saint in the spirit of greens!

Sunday Morning

In twilight
The blue hour takes center stage with its sensuous aura
Mission Bay waters
Smooth as a mirror
Reflect silhouettes of boats, houses, docks, trees
Soon fading as sunrise ascends in bright glory

That awesome sandcastle on the beach
Will soon be no more
When wind and water
Have their way

I walked along the shore
With a heart of gratitude for all I see
While memories of loved ones
Said hello to me

No doubt about this day of grace
Peace
Out there
Peace
Within me!
Praise be!

Artistic Journey

There it was
Like an exquisite painting
Lovingly crafted from found objects and pieces of a dream
A delightful gift of becoming

That giant gourd
Divided into a trio of parts
Reimagined by the artist, Apua Garbutt
With hidden hues of bright yellow flowers
And tones of orange, bronze, and black

Born of faith, imagination, and passion
Standing naked in the world
The mysterious, majestic presence
Whispering pregnant messages of femininity, sexuality,
Birth

The artist
Living with hope
Willing to risk all
By cutting it open
Just three days before the art exhibition
For a chance of creating a unique work of art
Straight from her heart

She answered the call
With focused intent
Offering her creation
With a sublime smile
To one and all

In the Silence

There they were
In the distance
Looking like silhouettes
Soundlessly walking on boardwalk
Through dense fog

On the beach
A young female quietly
Practices yoga poses
As waves of the sea
Roar to shore

Bark of trees
Shed their winter cloaks
While nearby shrubs
Reach for scant light
In hushed acts of change

Soul sister leans on restaurant wall
Waits alone
As motorists race by

Silence and sound
Existing on communal ground
What of the silence within?
What awesome gifts of Spirit exist
In the silence
Beyond the visible?

Joy
Peace
Love
Hope

Oh yes
They are there
Receiving me home!

A Christmas Moment in November

In dawn light
Snowflakes of last night
Cling to trees like a magical Christmas morn
The snow enticing memories
Of the winter wonderland at Yellowstone National Park
The surprise slowly melts away
Before my very eyes
A reminder to savor **NOW**
That's all we got!

Of Chicago Memories

Long ago
For the first time
I became acquainted with betrayal and grief
Like a snow-covered garden with no place to go
I hid within myself
Season after season
I lived with a broken heart

Slowly
I learned to trust again
Letting go of shame and blame
Understanding choice
Is the name of the game

When the winter of your life
Is all you have
Forgiveness offers the bright hope
Of a new beginning

Surrendering to the light of grace
I felt my heart open
With the joy of new space
For love

In Homage to Harriet Tubman

Harriet Tubman
Couldn't read nor write
Yet
She read the language of the stars
Shining brightly
Guided by faith and courage
Harriet found her way
From the South to the North

No No
She was not on a mountaintop
Like Moses of old
When she heard the call
But in the cotton kingdom
Among the thieves of humanity

When she answered
I shall be free
I shall be free
I must be free

For I am a child of the universe
Ordained by the creator to be free
I shall be free
I shall be free
I must be free

Because it is my birthright
Stolen from me
I shall be free
I shall be free
I must be free

For that is what life is to me
Free to be me
They tried to keep me in chains
No No
I am free
They gave me another name
No No
I am free

Ever mindful of freedom
She made a plan
With revolver in hand
To follow the North Star
Amid jet black skies

Spirit echoing
I shall be free
Mississippi River to cross
I shall be free
Hungry and thirsty
I shall be free
Walking through dense woodlands and treacherous
Swamps

I shall be free
Sleeping fits or not
I shall be free
Threats of death
I shall be free

Yes
She followed that guiding light
Getting help along the way
From near and far
In hidden places of the
Underground Railroad
To freedom land

"Now that I am free," said she
"I must go back
To bring slaves out of bondage
Into the marvelous light of freedom
So that they, too, will be free"

Free to live, work, and play
Free to love and marry their way
Free to have and keep their own children
Free to create new lives
With their own dreams
Free to decide when to get up or go to bed
Free to seek their daily bread
Free to face whatever lies ahead
Free to pray when Spirit leads

Free to build lives with their own deeds
Free to decide about their lives
Free to just be
Free
Free
Free

Harriet remembered well
When she asked the lord
To take her hand
Said she
"Twant me.
'Twas the Lord. I didn't know
Where to go or what to do but
I expected him to lead me
And he always did!"

Harriet Tubman
A giant of humanity

Thanks!

Music soothing my spirit with diverse rhythms
Thank you!
Art inspiring my imagination
With visions made visible
Thank you!
Flowers of countless hues
Adorn earth like none other
Thank you!
Living beings of all stripes interconnected as
One human family
Thank you!

On this Thanksgiving Day
Enshrined in America's culture
As a day of gratitude by President Abraham Lincoln
I hear the words
Thank you!
Taste and see abundant life
EVERYWHERE
Thank you!
Give thanks today and every day
Thankful for it all
It's the way to be!!!

Carry On

Sun of early morn
Pierces through gray clouds
Like a celestial eye
Watching the world go by

Sparse blue sky
Offers a tidbit of hope
For luminous glow to brighten today
And lift my spirit

Even when temporal circumstances
Of life say no
To this or that
Light is ever-present
Cloudy skies or not
To inspire me to be at peace
With whatever comes my way

Stolen Bike
Incredible Life

At age 12
Someone stole his brand new bike
He was mad as hell and ready to fight
A white policeman talked to him that day
And showed him another way
Leading him to a Louisville gym
Where he learned to become a skilled boxer

At age 18
He won the Olympic Gold Medal
That wasn't enough

He went on to win three championships
In the brutal business of professional boxing
That wasn't enough

He refused to be drafted into military service
To fight in a war of death and mayhem
He stood up for his religious beliefs with holy boldness
All the while saying
 "I ain't got no quarrel with them Vietcong"
That wasn't enough

Because he said no to that war call
He was stripped of his championships, fortune, and fame
Not allowed to fight in the prime of his game
That wasn't enough

His character thoroughly tested
In those dark days of strife
Sentenced to five years in prison
For rejecting the mandate to fight

Love
Not
Violence
Was his joy
Risking all
For a higher call

He stood his ground
No matter the cost
1200 days after jail decree
U.S. Supreme Court unanimously agreed
He had every right to honor his righteous creed

So he pressed on
Entering the ring once again
Older and wiser and so ready to please
Millions of fans
With rope-a-dope ease

He won back his championships as only he could do
Never once doubting that he would do it
Again
Again
And
Again
Saying all along "I am the greatest of them all"

His greatness was beyond the boxing ring
Touching hearts with words and deeds
Urging the masses everywhere
To claim their rights as worthy human beings

Civil Rights exemplar
Relentless protester
Tenacious spirit
Father, husband, friend, brother, too
Man of principle
Each day
Brand new

Embodiment of freedom
No three-fifth man
He
In the home of the brave and the land of the free

Free to speak his poetic words
Free to go where he was led
Free to be a global ambassador of peace
Free to stand for justice and equality
Free
To just to be
All the while declaring:
"I AM ALI"

Man of strength, power, and might
At age 42
He began another fight
That would test his courage beyond sight

Parkinson disease entered his body
And wouldn't go away
Staying for more than 30 years

Matters not that fate
He continued to run his race
With divine grace
Inspiring people worldwide
To rise to new heights
Regardless of their status in life

Oh yes
He crossed boundaries of faith and culture
Compassionate, humble, kind, and truthful
Perfectly clear about who he was
And
Whose he was

A generous child of the universe
Anointed by Allah
To be the beacon of hope
Demonstrating over and over
What is possible
When you truly believe

Oh
To be the giver of love
As he
For he was the greatest
Don't you see
Giving his all
So princely

Thank you
Muhammad Ali
For showing us the way
To be
THE GREATEST
By reflecting
The light of love
Each day

A Magical Morn

I waited for the words to come
To comfort my spirit after a short night of sleep

Dawn light reveals sky blue bay waters
Resting in quiet repose
The morning glow illuminates my way home

On crosswalk
A taupe brown dove
Struts with focused intent
Looking for nourishment
So do I
Of a different kind

At the seashore
I pause to inhale the salty air and
To witness waves
In endless motion

This mighty Pacific
Is my sanctuary
Inviting me to celebrate beauty
And to breathe!

Places

A Glimpse of Balboa Park

It was such a tender time of day
Soft light and hazy sky
My friend and I
Walking toward the entrance
Stopping to admire
Unusual shapes of two trees with
No leaves or signs of green life
Yet
Their barks
Twisted, gray, dry
Came alive as sculptured art

We entered a sensuous banquet of florals and sundry
Architecture
Showcasing cultural influences from around the world
The landscape aglow with colors galore
Red, yellow, purple, pink, blue, orange
And countless shrubs and trees

Kate Sessions saw the light of what could be done
To beautify barren land
When she long ago planted
1000 trees and multitudinous flowers from native plants
And seeds imported from around the world
With vision, commitment, dedication, and foresight
Recognized as the "Mother of Balboa Park"
Kate created a living legacy
A splendid oasis of peace
Amid the rush of city life

Iowa Morn

Frost of early morn
Clings to car windows like sparkling icy diamonds
Chilly winds sing winter's song of what's coming
Too soon

Distant vista exults luminosity
Blooming beyond autumn trees
Eye of heaven in radiant orange
Warms earth with light
Ever faithful to its purpose
Whatever the season

At Last!

Happy hearts
Far and near
Smile with glee
For the incredible achievement
Of the Chicago Cubs

Winners of
2016 World Series Championship
After a roller-coaster final game
Of rain delay
Ninth inning tie
And heart-stopping tenth

Long 68-year drought continues
For forlorn Cleveland Indians

While Cub fans revel
In magical aura
108 years in the making

Hurrah
Hurrah
Hurrah

For the Chicago Cubs
Winners of the grand trophy
At last!

A Winter Day in Chicago

Before dawn
Thick fog
Infuses atmosphere with murky gloom
Frosted trees sparkle
As snow clings to branches

Detours, delays, dissonance, dense traffic
Try to steal my tranquility

But I refuse to comply
As I recall my word of the day:
"Peace"
And my poem written long ago:
  "Oh
  How beautiful the day
  When peace abides
  Come what may"

  "Oh
  How beautiful this day
  When peace abides
  Come what may"

Peace
My partner amid the chaos
Blessing my day in every way

September Dawn

Autumn hues

Orange and yellow

Like a wall at the edge of a lake

Ascending sun

Shining

Shining

Shining

Appearing and disappearing

Amid morning haze

In a joyful dance of peek-a-boo!

The Power of Stillness

When I turned on my lamp
This morning
I noticed movement on the lampshade
A tiny spider rushing to the edge
To hide perfectly still

Was it pretending to be dead
Like a possum or salamander
Feeling threatened in the wilds?

Some animal behavior offers insights into stillness
They don't run away
But become still in the situation
In hope of survival

Stillness is my safe haven from the storms of my life
It's my way to evict anxieties and worries
As love opens my heart

Stillness is my oasis of
Peace

My soul speaks
Go there!
God is waiting!

Inquiry

Sea oh sea
What say thee to me?
Your sounds, movements
Will ever be

Sea oh sea
What say thee to me?
When my heart is heavy

Let it be!
Listen to the sounds of peace
See the cycles of change
Feel the breath of life
A gift to you and all!

Home

Is home a place?
Is it an address of an abode?
Is home the warmth of family and friends?
Is home that deep loving connection with a spouse?

What of a spiritual home?
Is it a sanctuary, a temple, a sacred haven amid the chaos
A place called heaven or eternal rest?

Is beauty home for my eyes?
Or listening to the sounds of the sea
Is that home for me, too?

I can remember countless times when I wanted to be near
The sea
I would travel to Martha's Vineyard, Nantucket Island,
Seattle, the Oregon Coast, San Diego
I felt at home as I walked along the sea

What of my emotional home of
Fears, anxieties, joys, anger, sadness, and countless other
Feelings
Coming and going like the waves of the sea
In the vicissitudes of my life

What does being home in my body feel like?
With those trillions of cells, organs, tissues
Or
The home of my mind
Where thoughts, dreams, imagination, ideas, and
Memories reside

Those palm trees along the side of the road
Transplanted long ago
Reaching for first light this morning
Are they at home in their new place known as San Diego?

When millions of people were taken from Africa
And enslaved on foreign shores over hundreds of years
Were they ever at home in body, mind, or spirit
In those alien new places?

For me
Home is a state of mind and a place where I live
It is being comfortable in my own skin
Just being me
Living my truth
Day by day
It is sharing time with family and friends
It is peace within
It is a sense of belonging
In the oneness of all creation
Yes, indeed
I am home
Wherever unconditional love is

Happy Life

I am a divine being imaged by God
Arriving on planet earth 75 years ago
Born into class, race, and social divides
Defined by people I did not know
Who decided to categorize and socialize me into their
World

Defined by narrow thoughts and ideas
Of some who did not know what they were doing
(Or maybe they did)
I bought into the illusions taught to me

Gradually

My body, mind, spirit, emotions, interactions, senses
Expanded my awareness of the uniqueness of me
I recognized color, energy, light, inner space and my
Intellect as guideposts for my imagination
I learned that I had the right to decide how to grow into
The person I have become
Wide awake to the truth that
Everything I have ever experienced informs this very moment

Yes

I have heard the stories of others on their journey of life
I have learned from them and so much more about ways
Traditions, customs, and how to have a better life

Yes

I have respect and deep gratitude for the gifts of nature
Great and small
The rich diversity, beauty, power and majestic forms
Inspire my heart
I realize that nature and I share a common bond
Of connectedness
For we are one in the fabric of life

Oh my
If that is true
(And I believe that it is)
Then I, too, am beautiful, powerful, majestic
Not because of where I live, or what I wear,
Or things I possess
But because I am a divine expression of creation
Plain and simple
A gift of love to the world

Thank God
I am not alone for
Each and every living being
Is born of that same love
Imagine that!

I am one with the divine
And so are you!

ACKNOWLEDGMENTS

I am grateful to all who gave me constant encouragement and generous support including Shirley J. Macklin, Loretta Brown, Ruby Dancy, Karen Snyder, Milton Webb, Lindsay McDonell, Barbara Holt, and Laura Farmer Sherman.

I also wish to thank my family, friends, and my NIA community in San Diego, California, who supported me on this journey. A special thanks to Lynn Winston, my book designer, and photographer, Leonid Tit.